The Ultimate

MARINADE

RECIPE BOOK

By
Les Ilagan

Les Ilagan

Copyright © CONTENT ARCADE PUBLISHING. All rights reserved.

This cookbook is copyright protected and meant for personal use only.

No part of this cookbook may be used, paraphrased, reproduced, scanned, distributed or sold in any printed or electronic form without permission of the author and the publishing company. Copying pages or any part of this book for any purpose other than own personal use is prohibited and would also mean violation of copyright law.

DISCLAIMER

Content Arcade Publishing and its authors are joined together in their efforts in creating these pages and their publications. Content Arcade Publishing and its authors make no assurance of any kind, stated or implied, with respect to the information provided.

LIMITS OF LIABILITY

Content Arcade Publishing and its authors shall not be held legally responsible in the event of incidental or consequential damages in line with, or arising out of, the supplying of the information presented here.

Table of Contents

Introduction 8

Homemade Chicken Satay Marinade 10

Easy Ceviche Marinade 12

Chili Garlic Marinade for Lamb Chops 14

Easy Chicken Tikka Masala Marinade 16

Easy Indian Spice Marinade 18

Mixed Herb Garlicand Oil Marinade 20

Lemon Oil and Garlic Marinade for Chicken 22

Marinara Sauce Marinade 24

Red Wine Vinegar Onion and Oregano Marinade 26

Yogurt with Garam Masala Marinade 28

Lemon Butter and Garlic Marinade with Rosemary 30

Spicy Chicken Marinade 32

Spicy Garlic Balsamic Marinade 34

Lemon with Ginger and HerbMarinade ...36

Spicy Tomato Marinade with Basil 38

Spicy Yogurt and Lemon Marinade 40

Garlic and Spice Marinade 42

Honey Lemon and Herb Marinade 44

Homemade Fajita Marinade 46

Easy Marinade for Chicken 48

Spiced Balsamic Maple Marinade.............50

Chili Lime Chicken Marinade....................52

Homemade Jerk Chicken Marinade 54

Parsley Garlic and Lemon Marinade........56

Honey Mustard and Garlic Marinade 58

Homemade Korean Chicken Barbecue Marinade 60

Mustard Yogurt Lamb Marinade 62

Red Curry Mayo Marinade 63

Easy Basil PestoMarinade 66

Easy Homemade Steak Marinade 68

Easy Teriyaki Marinade 70

Homemade Lemon Herb Marinade 72

Pepper Garlic and Oil Marinade 74

Homemade Chili Garlic Marinade 76

Tomato and Basil Marinade 78

The Ultimate Barbecue Marinade 80

Easy Satay Marinade 82

Chipotle Garlic Barbecue Marinade 84

Home-StyleSteak Marinade 86

Homemade Barbecue Marinade for Vegetables 88

Garlic Ginger and Cilantro Marinade 90

Easy Teriyaki Marinade 92

Spicy Vegetable Marinade..........................94

Soya Herb and Garlic Marinade................96

Spicy Grilled Chicken Marinade 98

Yogurt and Citrus Marinade with Coriander..100

Sweet and Spicy Barbecue Marinade 102

Lemon Ginger and Garlic Fish Marinade 104

Maple Lime and Herb Marinade 106

Sun-Dried Tomato Marinade with Garlic and Herb 108

INTRODUCTION

Cooking meat, fish, poultry, or vegetable by means of dry heat such as grilling, roasting, or baking can make them dry and would often taste bland without adequate seasoning. Marinating them is the perfect way to enhance the flavour and texture of your food.

This book will let you familiarize with the different kinds of condiments and how they can make your dishes taste even better.

This book provides you 50 different marinade recipes that you can use for marinating your fresh meat, poultry, fish, seafood and vegetables before cooking them.

Making your own marinades at home is very easy with the help of this book. It is also economical and would often require just a few basic ingredients that could already be in your pantry, so all the more reason not to go for commercially-prepared marinades.

This book will come handy whether you are making dinner for the family or planning for a weekend barbecue party. With the easy-to-follow instructions, you'll find that working with these recipes could be as easy as one-two-three.

This book is a part of many cookbook series that I am writing, I hope you have fun trying all the recipes in this book.

So now, let's get it started!

Les Ilagan

Homemade Chicken Satay Marinade

A wonderful Asian-inspired marinade recipe that highlights the flavor of coconut milk, peanuts and curry.

Preparation time: 5 minutes
Total time: 5 minutes
Yield: 1 1/4 cups

Ingredients
2/3 cup coconut milk

1/3 cup creamy peanut butter
3 cloves garlic, minced
2 tablespoons brown sugar
2 tablespoons lime or lemon juice
2 tablespoons fresh chives (chopped)
1 teaspoon soy sauce
1 teaspoon curry powder
salt and freshly ground black pepper

Method

1. Whisk together the coconut milk, peanut butter, garlic cloves, brown sugar, lime juice, chives, soy sauce, and curry powder in a small bowl until blended well.

2. Season with salt and pepper, to taste.

3. Now, the marinade is ready to use.

4. Simply add the mixture onto your chicken or meatslices and marinate for at least 2 hours.

♦♦♦♦♦♦♦♦

Easy Ceviche Marinade

This is the best marinade for your fresh seafood. Totally delicious!

Preparation Time: 10minutes
Total Time: 10 minutes
Yield: 1 ¼ cup

Ingredients
1 cup lime juice
2 tablespoons olive oil
1 shallot (minced)
3 green onions (minced)
1 stalk celery (minced)
1 tablespoon cilantro (minced)

1 minced red hot chili pepper (optional)
salt and freshly ground black pepper

Method
1. In a small bowl, combine the lime juice, olive oil, shallot, green onions, celery, cilantro, and chili. Mix well. Season with salt and pepper, to taste.
2. Now, the marinade ready to use.
3. Pour the mixture onto your fresh fish or seafood and marinate for at least 1-2 hours or until seafood becomes opaque.

♦♦♦♦♦♦♦♦

Les Ilagan

Chili Garlic Marinade for Lamb Chops

If you are looking for a spicy marinade to go with your grilled lamb chops, this is the perfect recipe for you!

Preparation time: 5 minutes
Total time: 5 minutes
Yield: 1 cup

Ingredients
2/3 cup red wine vinegar
1/3 cup olive oil

1 teaspoon chili powder
1 teaspoon garlic (minced)
1/2 teaspoon of cumin, ground
1/2 teaspoon of salt
1/2 teaspoon of ground black pepper

Method

1. Combine the red wine vinegar, olive oil, chili powder, garlic, cumin, salt and pepper in a bowl. Mix them together really well.

2. Now, the marinade is ready to use.

3. Add mixture onto your lamb chops and marinate for at least 2 hours.

♦♦♦♦♦♦♦♦♦

Les Ilagan

Easy Chicken Tikka Masala Marinade

This creamy and spicy marinade recipe is bursting with wonderful flavors.

Preparation time: 5minutes
Total Time: 5 minutes
Yield: 1 cup

Ingredients

1 cup Greek yogurt
2 tablespoons lemon juice
1 tablespoon fresh ginger (minced)

2 teaspoons cumin (ground)
2 teaspoons cayenne pepper
1 teaspoon cinnamon (ground)
salt and freshly ground black pepper

Method

1. Combine the yogurt, lemon juice, ginger, cumin, cayenne pepper, and cinnamon in a small bowl. Season with salt and pepper, to taste. Mix them together really well.

2. Now, the marinade is ready to use.

3. Add mixture onto your meat and marinate for at least 1-2 hours.

◆◆◆◆◆◆◆◆◆

Les Ilagan

Easy Indian Spice Marinade

A nice, spicy take on the traditional Indian marinade for chicken, fish, or meat!

Preparation time: 5 minutes
Total time: 5 minutes
Yield: 1 ¼ cups

Ingredients
1 cup Greek yogurt
2 tablespoons lemon juice
3 cloves of garlic (minced)

1 medium onion (finely chopped)
2 teaspoon cayenne pepper
1 teaspoon turmeric (ground)
1 teaspoon cumin (ground)
1 teaspoon cinnamon (ground)
1 teaspoon paprika
salt and freshly ground black pepper

Method

1. Combine the yogurt, lemon juice, garlic, onion, cayenne pepper, turmeric, cumin, cinnamon, and paprika in a small bowl. Season with salt and pepper, to taste. Mix them together really well.

2. Now, the marinade is ready to use.

3. Add mixture onto your chicken, fish, or meat and marinate for at least 1-2 hours to absorb flavors.

♦♦♦♦♦♦♦♦♦

Les Ilagan

Mixed Herb Garlic and Oil Marinade

Marinating your meat with mixed herbs is the best way to add flavor naturally. This is a versatile recipe that can go well with meat, fish, or chicken.

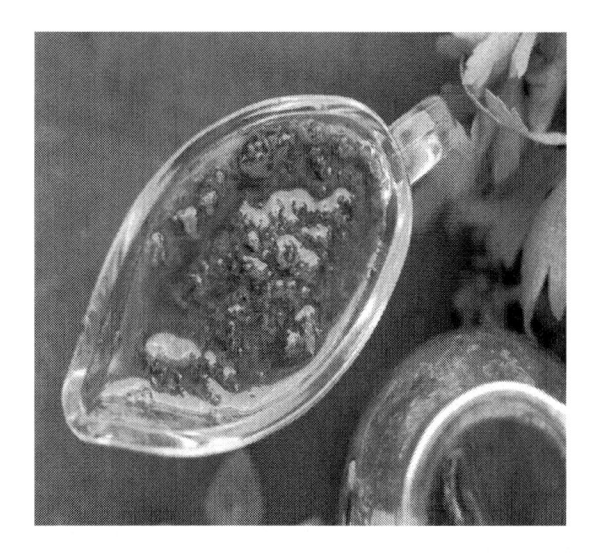

Preparation Time: 5 minutes
Total Time: 5 minutes
Yield: 1 ¼ cups

Ingredients
1 cup olive oil
2 tablespoons lemon juice or lime juice

3 cloves garlic (minced)
2 tablespoons fresh parsley (finely chopped)
1 tablespoon fresh basil (finely chopped)
1 tablespoon fresh thyme (finely chopped)
salt and freshly ground black pepper

Method

1. Whisk together the oil, lemon juice, garlic, parsley, basil, and thyme in a small bowl. Season with salt and pepper, to taste. Mix them really well.

2. Now, the marinade is ready to use.

3. Simply add mixture onto your meat, fish, or chicken and marinate for at least 1-2 hours to absorb flavors.

◆◆◆◆◆◆◆◆◆

Lemon Oil and Garlic Marinade for Chicken

This marinade recipe is very simple yet very flavorful!

Preparation time: 5minutes
Total time: 5 minutes
Yield: 1 ¼ cups

Ingredients

1 cup extra-virgin olive oil
¼ cup of lemon juice
3 cloves of garlic (pressed)

1 tablespoon of lemon zest (finely grated)
1 tablespoon of fresh rosemary (chopped)
salt and freshly ground black pepper

Method

1. Whisk together the oil, lemon juice, garlic, zest, and rosemary in a small bowl. Season with salt and pepper, to taste. Mix them really well.
2. Now, the marinade is ready to use.
3. Add mixture onto your meat, fish, or chicken and marinate for at least 1-2 hours to absorb flavors.

♦♦♦♦♦♦♦♦♦

Les Ilagan

Marinara Sauce Marinade

This delicious marinade is perfect for fish or even chicken.

Preparation time: 5 minutes
Total time: 5 minutes
Yield: 1 1/4 cups

Ingredients
½ cup tomato puree
½ cup olive oil

1 medium lime (juiced)
½ cup of onion (diced)
3 cloves garlic
1 tablespoon of fresh parsley (finely chopped)
1 teaspoon dried oregano
1 teaspoon dried basil
salt and freshly ground black pepper

Method

1. Whisk together the tomato puree, olive oil, lime juice, onion, garlic, parsley, oregano, and basil in a small bowl. Season with salt and pepper, to taste. Mix them really well.
2. Now, the marinade is ready to use.
3. **Add mixture onto your fish or chicken and marinate for at least 1-2 hours to absorb flavors.**

♦♦♦♦♦♦♦♦♦

Les Ilagan

Red Wine Vinegar Onion and Oregano Marinade

This is a great tasting marinade that is perfect for meat, chicken, fish, and even vegetables.

Preparation time: 5 minutes
Total time: 5 minutes
Yield: 1 cup

Ingredients

1/2 cup red wine vinegar
1/3 cup dry red wine
2 tablespoon olive oil

1/4 cup fresh oregano (cut into small pieces)
1 large onion (thinly sliced)
1 tablespoon of whole peppercorns
2 cloves of garlic (minced)
salt and freshly ground black pepper

Method

1. Combine together the red wine vinegar, dry red wine, olive oil, oregano, onion, peppercorns, and garlic in a small bowl. Season with salt and pepper, to taste. Mix them really well.
2. Now, the marinade is ready to use.
3. Pour mixture onto your meat, chicken, fish or vegetable and marinate for at least 1-2 hours to absorb flavors.

♦♦♦♦♦♦♦♦♦

Les Ilagan

Yogurt with Garam Masala Marinade

This awesome marinade recipe is can be used for marinating lamb, beef, or chicken.

Preparation time: 5minutes
Total time: 5 minutes
Yield: 1 1/4 cups

Ingredients
1 cup plain yogurt
3 tablespoons olive oil
2 teaspoons garam masala

2 cloves garlic (minced)
1 shallot (minced)
2 teaspoons ginger (freshly grated)
salt and freshly ground black pepper

Method

1. Combine together the yogurt, olive oil, garam masala, garlic, and ginger in a small bowl. Season with salt and pepper, to taste. Mix them thoroughly.
2. Now, the marinade is ready to use.
3. Pour mixture onto your meat, chicken, fish or vegetable and marinate for at least 1-2 hours to absorb flavors.

◆◆◆◆◆◆◆◆◆

Lemon Butter and Garlic Marinade with Rosemary

Add a fresh flavor to your grilled meat dishes with this wonderful marinade.

Preparation time: 5 minutes
Total time: 5 minutes
Yield: 1 cup

Ingredients

2 medium lemon (juiced and zested)
½ cup butter melted

2 cloves garlic (minced)
2 tablespoons fresh rosemary, chopped
salt and freshly ground black pepper

Method

1. Combine together the lemon juice, zest, butter, garlic, and rosemary in a small bowl. Season with salt and pepper, to taste. Mix them thoroughly.
2. Now, the marinade is ready to use.
3. Pour mixture onto your meat and marinate for at least 1-2 hours to absorb flavors.

♦♦♦♦♦♦♦♦♦

Spicy Chicken Marinade

This spicy marinade recipe is perfect for grilled chicken or ribs.

Preparation time: 5 minutes
Total time: 5 minutes
Yield: 1 cup

Ingredients

3/4 cup ketchup
1/3 cup vinegar
1/4 cup onion(finely chopped)

2 cloves garlic (minced)
2 tablespoons vegetable oil
1 tablespoon Worcestershire sauce
1 tablespoon brown sugar
1 teaspoon dry mustard
1 teaspoon chili powder or cayenne pepper
1/2 teaspoon cumin (ground)
1/2 teaspoon salt
1/2 teaspoon black pepper

Method

1. Combine together ketchup, vinegar, onion, garlic, oil, Worcestershire sauce, brown sugar, mustard, chili powder, and cumin in a small bowl. Season with salt and pepper, to taste. Mix them thoroughly.

2. Now, the marinade is ready to use.

3. Pour mixture onto your chicken and marinate for at least 1-2 hours to absorb flavors.

♦♦♦♦♦♦♦♦

Les Ilagan

Spicy Garlic Balsamic Marinade

This spicy marinade is can be used to any kind of meat.

Preparation time: 5 minutes
Total time: 5 minutes
Yield: 1 cup

Ingredients
1/2 cup balsamic vinegar
1/2 cup olive oil

3 cloves garlic (minced)
1 red hot chili pepper (chopped)
1/2 teaspoon salt
1/2 teaspoon black pepper

Method
1. Whisk together balsamic vinegar, olive oil, garlic, and chili in a small bowl. Season with salt and pepper, to taste. Mix them thoroughly.
2. Now, the marinade is ready to use.
3. Pour mixture onto your choice of meat and marinate for at least 1-2 hours to absorb flavors.

♦♦♦♦♦♦♦♦

Les Ilagan

Lemon with Ginger and Herb Marinade

This fantastic marinade recipe is perfect for marinating fish or poultry.

Preparation time: 5 minutes
Total time: 5 minutes
Yield: 1 cup

Ingredients

1/2 cup lemon juice
1/3 cup olive oil

2 tablespoon ginger juice
1/4 cup fresh mixed herbs (chopped)
salt and freshly ground black pepper

Method

1. Whisk together lemon juice, olive oil, ginger juice, and mixed herbs in a small bowl. Season with salt and pepper, to taste. Mix them thoroughly.

2. Now, the marinade is ready to use.

3. Pour mixture onto your choice of meat and marinate for at least 1-2 hours to absorb flavors.

♦♦♦♦♦♦♦♦♦

Les Ilagan

Spicy Tomato Marinade with Basil

This spicy tomato marinade is very easy to prepare and only needs a few basic ingredients.

Preparation Time: 5 minutes
Total Time: 5 minutes
Yield: 1 cup

Ingredients

2/3 cup tomato puree
1/3 cup olive oil
2 tablespoons lemon juice
1 teaspoon dried basil
1 teaspoon cayenne pepper

1 teaspoon paprika
salt and freshly ground black pepper

Method

1. In a small bowl, combine the tomato puree, olive oil, lemon juice, basil, cayenne pepper and paprika. Season with salt and pepper, to taste. Mix them thoroughly.
2. Now, the marinade is ready to use.
3. Pour mixture onto your choice of meat and marinate for at least 1-2 hours to absorb flavors.

♦♦♦♦♦♦♦♦♦

Les Ilagan

Spicy Yogurt and Lemon Marinade

This marinade with yogurt, lemon, and chili will give you a tender grilled meat with awesome flavor.

Preparation time: 5 minutes
Total time: 5 minutes
Yield: 1 1/4 cups

Ingredients
1 cup Greek yogurt
2 tablespoons lemon juice

2 tablespoons onion (finely chopped)
2 cloves garlic (minced)
1 teaspoon sweet paprika
1 teaspoon chili powder
1 teaspoon cumin (ground)
1 teaspoon of white sugar
salt and freshly ground black pepper

Method

1. In a small bowl, combine the yogurt, lemon juice, onion, garlic, paprika, chili powder, cumin, and sugar. Season with salt and pepper, to taste. Mix them thoroughly.

2. Now, the marinade is ready to use.

3. Pour mixture onto your choice of meat and marinate for at least 1-2 hours to absorb flavors.

◆◆◆◆◆◆◆◆◆

Les Ilagan

Garlic and Spice Marinade

Simple yet flavorful marinade recipe for your roasted chicken.

Preparation time: 5 minutes
Total Time: 5 minutes
Yield: 1 cup

Ingredients

½ cup olive oil
½ cup lemon juice
4 cloves garlic (minced)

1 teaspoon sweet paprika
1 teaspoon chili powder
1 teaspoon coriander seed (ground)
1 teaspoon of brown sugar
salt and freshly ground black pepper

Method

1. In a small bowl, whisk together the olive oil, lemon juice, garlic, paprika, chili powder, coriander, and brown sugar. Season with salt and pepper, to taste. Mix them thoroughly.
2. Now, the marinade is ready to use.
3. Pour mixture onto your chicken and marinate for at least 1-2 hours to absorb flavors.

◆◆◆◆◆◆◆◆

Les Ilagan

Honey Lemon and Herb Marinade

A sweet and tangy marinade with honey, lemon, olive oil, and fresh herbs. It is great for chicken, fish, or seafood.

Preparation time: 5 minutes
Total time: 5 minutes
Yield: 1 cup

Ingredients

2 medium lemons (juiced)

Marinade Recipe Book

1/4 cup olive oil
1/4 cup honey
1/4 cup fresh mixed herbs
1/2 teaspoon salt
1/4 teaspoon ground black pepper

Method

1. In a small bowl, whisk together the lemon juice, olive oil, honey, and mixed herbs. Season with salt and pepper, to taste.
2. Now, the marinade is ready to use.
3. **Pour** mixture onto your meat or chicken and marinate for at least 1-2 hours to absorb flavors.

◆◆◆◆◆◆◆◆

Les Ilagan

Homemade Fajita Marinade

This fajita marinade recipe made with soy sauce, lime juice, olive oil and spices is so delicious. It can be used for either meat or chicken.

Preparation Time: 5 minutes
Total Time: 5 minutes
Yield: 3/4 cup

Ingredients

1/2 cup lime juice
1/4 cup olive oil
4 cloves garlic (minced)

2 tablespoons soy sauce
1 teaspoon brown sugar
1/2 teaspoon liquid smoke flavoring
1/2 teaspoon cayenne pepper
1/2 teaspoon cumin (ground)
1/2 teaspoon coriander (ground)
salt and freshly ground black pepper

Method
1. In a small bowl, combine the lime juice, olive oil, garlic, soy sauce, brown sugar, liquid smoke flavouring, cayenne pepper, cumin, and coriander. Season with salt and pepper, to taste. Mix them thoroughly.
2. Now, the marinade is ready to use.
3. Pour mixture onto your meat or chicken and marinate for at least 1-2 hours to absorb flavors.

◆◆◆◆◆◆◆◆

Les Ilagan

Easy Marinade for Chicken

Bring more flavor to your grilled chicken with this easy and tasty marinade recipe.

Preparation Time: 5minutes
Total Time: 5 minutes
Yield: 1 cup

Ingredients
2/3 cup olive oil
1/3 cup apple cider vinegar
1 teaspoon dry mustard
1 teaspoon Worcestershire sauce
1 teaspoon of caraway seeds(ground)

1 teaspoon honey
salt and freshly ground black pepper, to taste

Method

1. In a small bowl, combine the olive oil, apple cider vinegar, dry mustard, Worcestershire sauce, caraway, and honey. Season with salt and pepper, to taste. Mix them thoroughly.
2. Now, the marinade is ready to use.
3. Pour mixture onto your chicken and marinate for at least 1-2 hours to absorb flavors.

♦♦♦♦♦♦♦♦

Les Ilagan

Spiced Balsamic Maple Marinade

A great tasting marinade for your grilled steaks, this is so good that you'd want to have some more.

Preparation time: 5 minutes
Total time: 5 minutes
Yield: 1 cup

Ingredients

1/3 cup olive oil
1/3 cup balsamic vinegar

2 tablespoons maple syrup
1 teaspoon paprika
1 teaspoon cumin (ground)
1 teaspoon cayenne pepper
salt and freshly ground black pepper

Method

1. In a small bowl, combine the olive oil, balsamic vinegar, maple syrup, paprika, cumin, and cayenne pepper. Season with salt and pepper, to taste. Mix them thoroughly.
2. Now, the marinade is ready to use.
3. Pour mixture onto your chicken and marinate for at least 1-2 hours to absorb flavors.

♦♦♦♦♦♦♦♦

Les Ilagan

Chili Lime Chicken Marinade

This spicy marinade works well with grilled chicken.

Preparation time: 5 minutes
Total time: 5 minutes
Yield: 1cup

Ingredients

1/2 cup olive oil
1/2 cupfreshly squeezed lime juice
1 shallot (finely chopped)
4 garlic cloves (minced)

1 teaspoon chili powder
1 teaspoon coriander seed (ground)
salt and freshly ground black pepper

Method

1. In a small bowl, combine the lime juice, olive oil, shallot, garlic, chili powder, and coriander. Season with salt and pepper, to taste. Mix them thoroughly.
2. Now, the marinade is ready to use.
3. Pour mixture onto your chicken and marinate for at least 1-2 hours to absorb flavors.

♦♦♦♦♦♦♦♦♦

Les Ilagan

Homemade Jerk Chicken Marinade

This awesome grilled jerk chicken marinade recipe is very easy to make and so yummy!

Preparation time: 5 minutes
Total time: 5 minutes
Yield: 1 cup

Ingredients

1/2 cup olive oil
1/3 cup fresh lime juice
2 tablespoons soy sauce
3 scallions

4 large garlic cloves
1 medium onion (quartered)
3 Scotch bonnet or habanero chili(stemmed and seeded)
1 tablespoon brown sugar
1 tablespoon fresh thyme leaves
1 teaspoon allspice (ground)
1 teaspoon nutmeg (freshly grated)
1 teaspoon cinnamon (ground)
1 teaspoon salt
1 teaspoon black pepper (ground)

Method

1. Combine the olive oil, lime juice, soy sauce, scallions, garlic, onion, chili, brown sugar, and thyme in a food processor or blender. Process until smooth.

2. Add the all spice, nutmeg, cinnamon, salt and pepper. Blend further 5 seconds.

3. Now, the marinade is ready to use.

4. Pour mixture onto your chicken and marinate for at least 1-2 hours to absorb flavors.

◆◆◆◆◆◆◆◆

Les Ilagan

Parsley Garlic and Lemon Marinade

This is a quick and easy marinade recipe for chicken, fish, or seafood.

Preparation time: 5 minutes
Total time: 5 minutes
Yield: 1 cup

Ingredients

2/3 cup of olive oil
1/3 cup lemon juice
3 tablespoons fresh parsley (chopped)

1 teaspoon of lemon zest (finely grated)
3 cloves of garlic (finely chopped)
salt and freshly ground black pepper

Method

1. In a small bowl, combine the olive oil, lemon juice, parsley, lemon zest, and garlic. Season with salt and pepper, to taste. Mix them thoroughly.
2. Now the marinade is ready to use.
3. Pour mixture onto your chicken, fish or seafood and marinate for at least 1-2 hours to absorb flavors.

◆◆◆◆◆◆◆◆

Honey Mustard and Garlic Marinade

This marinade recipe with honey, mustard, and garlic is great for roasted, baked or grilled chicken or fish.

Preparation time: 5 minutes
Total time: 5 minutes
Yield: 1 cup

Ingredients
3/4cup of mayonnaise

2 tablespoons honey
2 tablespoons Dijon mustard
1 tablespoon Worcestershire sauce
1 teaspoon garlic (minced)
salt and freshly ground black pepper

Method

1. In a small bowl, combine the mayonnaise, honey, Dijon mustard, Worcestershire sauce, and garlic. Season with salt and pepper, to taste. Mix them thoroughly.
2. Now, the marinade is ready to use.
3. Pour mixture onto your chicken or fish and marinate for at least 1-2 hours to absorb flavors.

♦♦♦♦♦♦♦♦

Homemade Korean Chicken Barbecue Marinade

If you want a spicy and flavorful marinade for your chicken, this is the recipe for you!

Preparation time: 5 minutes
Total time: 5 minutes
Yield: 2 ½ cups

Ingredients
3/4 cup soy sauce
3/4 cup water
3/4 cup brown sugar
1/4cup of rice vinegar

1 tablespoon hot chili paste
1 teaspoon ground ginger
1 teaspoon onion powder
1 teaspoon garlic powder
1 teaspoon sesame oil

Method

1. Whisk together the soy sauce, water, brown sugar, and rice vinegar in a small saucepan. Bring to a boil over high heat. Reduce heat and simmer for 5 minutes. Remove from heat.
2. Stir in the chili paste, ginger, onion powder, garlic powder, and sesame oil.Allow to cool.
3. Now, the marinade is ready to use.
4. Pour mixture onto your chicken and marinate for at least 1-2 hours to absorb flavors.

♦♦♦♦♦♦♦♦♦

Les Ilagan

Mustard Yogurt Lamb Marinade

This is the perfect marinade recipe for lamb chops. Guaranteed to satisfy those hungry tummies!

Preparation time: 5 minutes
Total time: 5 minutes
Yield: 1 1/3 cups

Ingredients
1 cup Greek yogurt
4 tablespoon wholegrain mustard

2 tablespoons lemon juice
1 tablespoon fresh mixed herbs (chopped)
1 tablespoon honey
salt and freshly ground black pepper

Method

1. Combine the yogurt, wholegrain mustard, lemon juice, mixed herbs, and honey in a small bowl. Season with salt and pepper, to taste. Mix well.
2. Now, the marinade is ready to use.
3. Pour mixture onto your lamb chops and marinate for at least 1-2 hours to absorb flavors.

♦♦♦♦♦♦♦♦

Red Curry Mayo Marinade

Les Ilagan

This marinade recipe with red curry and mayonnaise is perfect for roasted poultry, fish, or meat!

Preparation time: 5 minutes
Total time: 5 minutes
Yield: 1 cup

Ingredients

1 cup of mayonnaise
2 tablespoons of lemon juice
1 tablespoon of honey
1 teaspoon of red curry powder
1 teaspoon garlic powder
salt and freshly ground black pepper

Method
1. Mix together mayonnaise, lemon juice, honey, red curry powder, and garlic powder in a small bowl. Stir until combined well. Season with salt and pepper, to taste.
2. Now, the marinade is ready to use.
3. Pour mixture onto your poultry, fish, or meat and marinate for at least 1-2 hours to absorb flavors.

♦♦♦♦♦♦♦♦

Les Ilagan

Easy Basil Pesto Marinade

Your favorite pasta sauce for marinade? Yes you can! Just follow this easy awesome recipe!

Preparation time: 5 minutes
Total time: 5 minutes
Yield: 1 2/3 cups

Ingredients

2cups fresh basil leaves (finely chopped)
3 cloves garlic (minced)
¼ cup pine nuts
1 cup of olive oil

2 tablespoons lemon juice
salt and freshly ground black pepper

Method

1. Combine basil, garlic, pine nuts in a blender or food processor. Pulse until it forms a paste.

2. Add olive oil bit by bit while motor is running. Season with salt and pepper, to taste.

3. Now, the marinade is ready to use.

4. Pour mixture onto your poultry, fish, or meat and marinate for at least 1-2 hours to absorb flavors.

♦♦♦♦♦♦♦♦

Les Ilagan

Easy Homemade Steak Marinade

This steak marinade with red wine vinegar, olive oil and bay leaves is very easy to make and delicious.

Preparation time: 5 minutes
Total time: 5 minutes
Yield: 1 1/3 cup

Ingredients
2/3 cup olive oil

2/3 cup red wine vinegar
3cloves garlic (minced)
1 tablespoon brown sugar
1 teaspoon sweet paprika
4 bay leaves (crushed)
salt and freshly ground black pepper

Method

1. Mix together the oil, red wine vinegar, garlic, brown sugar, and paprika in a small bowl. Stir until combined well. Season with salt and pepper, to taste. Add the bay leaves.

2. Now, the marinade is ready to use.

3. Pour mixture onto your meat and marinate for at least 1-2 hours to absorb flavors.

♦♦♦♦♦♦♦♦

Easy Teriyaki Marinade

This Asian-inspired marinade recipe goes well with either beef or chicken!

Preparation time: 5 minutes
Total time: 5 minutes
Yield: 1 2/3 cups

Ingredients

1/2 cup soy sauce
1/2 cup mirin
1/2 cup rice wine vinegar

2 tablespoons brown sugar
1 teaspoon ginger juice
2 teaspoons cornstarch
2 tablespoons water

Method

1. In a small saucepan, whisk together the soy sauce, mirin, rice wine, brown sugar, and ginger juice. Bring to a boil over high heat.
2. Combine cornstarch and water in a small bowl. Stir until dissolved. Pour into the saucepan. Cook for 2-3 minutes, stirring constantly. Allow to cool.
3. Now, the marinade is ready to use.
4. Pour mixture onto your meat and marinate for at least 1-2 hours to absorb flavors.

♦♦♦♦♦♦♦♦

Les Ilagan

Homemade Lemon Herb Marinade

This is a basic marinade recipe that goes well with any kind of meat.

Preparation time: 5 minutes
Total time: 5 minutes
Yield: 3/4 cup

Ingredients

1/2cuplemon juice
1/4 cup olive oil
2 tablespoons fresh parsley (finely chopped)

1/2 teaspoon of dried oregano
1/2teaspoon of dried basil
1/2teaspoon of garlic powder
1/2 teaspoon of paprika
salt and freshly ground black pepper

Method

1. Combine the lemon juice, olive oil, and mixed herbs in a small bowl. Season with salt and pepper, to taste. Mix well.
2. Now, the marinade is ready to use.
3. Pour mixture onto your lamb chops and marinate for at least 1-2 hours to absorb flavors.

◆◆◆◆◆◆◆◆

Les Ilagan

Pepper Garlic and Oil Marinade

A super easy marinade that calls for a few basic ingredients.

Preparation time: 5 minutes
Total time: 5 minutes
Yield: 2/3 cup

Ingredients
1/2 cup olive oil
2 tablespoons apple cider vinegar

1 tablespoon garlic (minced)
1 teaspoon coriander seed (ground)
1/2 teaspoon Kosher salt
1/2 teaspoon freshly ground black pepper

Method

1. Combine the olive oil, apple cider vinegar, garlic, coriander, salt, and pepper in a small bowl. Mix well.
2. Now, the marinade is ready to use.
3. Pour mixture onto your poultry, meat, or fish and marinate for at least 1-2 hours to absorb flavors.

◆◆◆◆◆◆◆◆

Homemade Chili Garlic Marinade

Super-hot! This spicy marinade will give your grilled meat dishes that kick that you desired.

Preparation time: 5 minutes
Total time: 5 minutes
Yield: 1 cup

Ingredients

2/3 cup red wine vinegar
1/3 cup olive oil
3 cloves garlic (minced)

2 teaspoons chili paste
1 teaspoon cumin powder
1 teaspoon paprika
1/2 teaspoon of all-spice
salt and freshly ground black pepper

Method

1. Whisk together the red wine vinegar, olive oil, garlic, chili paste, cumin powder, and paprika in a small bowl. Season with salt and pepper, to taste. Mix well.

2. Now, the marinade is ready to use.

3. Pour mixture onto your poultry, meat, or fish and marinate for at least 1-2 hours to absorb flavors.

♦♦♦♦♦♦♦♦

Tomato and Basil Marinade

So easy to make and definitely delicious, this marinade goes well with chicken, fish, or seafood.

Preparation time: 5 minutes
Total time: 5 minutes
Yield: 1 cup

Ingredients
2/3 cup olive oil
1/3 cup tomato puree
2 tablespoons fresh basil (finely chopped)

1 teaspoon garlic powder
1 teaspoon sweet paprika
1/2 teaspoon of salt
1/2 teaspoon of freshly ground black pepper

Method

1. In a small saucepan over medium-high heat, heat the olive oil. Add in the tomato puree and dry white wine let it cook for 10 minutes.

2. Stir in the basil, garlic powder, paprika, salt, and pepper. Remove from heat. Allow to cool.

3. Now, the marinade is ready to use.

4. Pour mixture onto your poultry, meat, or fish and marinate for at least 1-2 hours to absorb flavors.

♦♦♦♦♦♦♦♦

Les Ilagan

The Ultimate Barbecue Marinade

This is the best marinade for any barbecue. So simple and easy to make!

Preparation time: 5 minutes
Total time: 5 minutes
Yield: 1 cup

Ingredients

1/3 cup ketchup
1/3 cup brown sugar
1/3 cup soy sauce

1 tablespoon Worcestershire sauce
1 teaspoon garlic powder
1 teaspoon onion powder
1 teaspoon paprika
1 teaspoon hot pepper sauce
1 teaspoon cumin (ground)

Method

1. Whisk together the ketchup, brown sugar, soy sauce, Worcestershire sauce, garlic powder, onion powder, paprika, hot pepper sauce, and cumin in a small bowl. Mix well.

2. Now, the marinade is ready to use.

3. Pour mixture onto your poultry, meat, or fish and marinate for at least 1-2 hours to absorb flavors.

♦♦♦♦♦♦♦♦

Les Ilagan

Easy Satay Marinade

This dish is popular in Asia where chicken is marinated in a flavorful peanut sauce!

Preparation time: 5 minutes
Total time: 5 minutes
Yield: 1 cup

Ingredients

1/2 cups of coconut milk
1/4 cup peanut butter
2 tablespoons lime juice
2 cloves garlic (minced)

2 teaspoons kekapmanis
1 teaspoon curry paste
1 teaspoon sugar
1 teaspoon chili powder (optional)
salt and freshly ground black pepper

Method

1. Combine together the coconut milk, peanut butter, lime juice, garlic, kekapmanis, curry paste, sugar, and chili powder in a small bowl. Season with salt and pepper, to taste. Mix well.
2. Now, the marinade is ready to use.
3. Pour mixture onto your chicken or meat and marinate for at least 1-2 hours to absorb flavors.

◆◆◆◆◆◆◆◆

Les Ilagan

Chipotle Garlic Barbecue Marinade

A sweet and spicy barbecue marinade recipe.

Preparation time: 5 minutes
Total time: 5 minutes
Yield:1 ¼ cups

Ingredients

1/2 cup ketchup
1/2 cup maple syrup
2 tablespoons olive oil
2 tablespoons soy sauce

1 tablespoon Worcestershire sauce
2 teaspoons garlic (chopped)
2 chipotle chilies (minced)

Method

1. Whisk together the ketchup, maple syrup, olive oil, soy sauce, Worcestershire sauce, garlic, and chillies in a small bowl. Mix well.
2. Now, the marinade is ready to use.
3. Pour mixture onto your poultry, meat, or fish and marinate for at least 1-2 hours to absorb flavors.

◆◆◆◆◆◆◆◆

Les Ilagan

Home-Style Steak Marinade

This is a fantastic marinade for your steaks and chicken.

Preparation time: 5 minutes
Total time: 5 minutes
Yield: 1 cup

Ingredients

1/4 cup tomato sauce
1/4 cup soy sauce
1/4 cup brown sugar
2 tablespoons Worcestershire sauce

2 tablespoons apple cider vinegar
3-4 drops hot pepper sauce
1 teaspoon cumin (ground)
1 teaspoon sweet paprika
1/2 teaspoon Koshersalt
1/2 teaspoon freshly ground black pepper

Method

1. In a small bowl, whisk together the ketchup, soy sauce, brown sugar, Worcestershire sauce, apple cider vinegar, hot pepper sauce, cumin, paprika, salt and pepper.

2. Now, the marinade is ready to use.

3. Pour mixture onto your poultry, meat, or fish and marinate for at least 1-2 hours to absorb flavors.

♦♦♦♦♦♦♦♦

Les Ilagan

Homemade Barbecue Marinade for Vegetables

Perfect marinade for grilled vegetables. Delicious, just what you need for outdoor barbecue parties.

Preparation time: 5 minutes
Total time: 5 minutes
Yield: 3/4 cup

Ingredients
1/4 cup balsamic vinegar

2 tablespoons olive oil
2 table spoons soy sauce
2 table spoons brown sugar
1 teaspoon molasses
1 teaspoon of wholegrain mustard
1/2 teaspoon of onion powder
1/2 teaspoon of garlic powder
1/2 teaspoon freshly ground black pepper

Method

1. In a small bowl, combine the balsamic vinegar, olive oil, soy sauce, brown sugar, molasses, mustard, onion powder, garlic powder, and pepper. Mix well.
2. Now, the marinade is ready to use.
3. Pour mixture onto your vegetables and marinate for at least 1-2 hours to absorb flavors.

♦♦♦♦♦♦♦♦

Garlic Ginger and Cilantro Marinade

This has become a family favorite. It's great on chicken or fish particularly salmon and tuna.

Preparation Time: 5 minutes
Total Time: 5 minutes
Yield: 1 cup

Ingredients
2/3 cup white wine
1/3 cup olive oil
1 teaspoon fresh ginger root (minced)
1 teaspoon garlic (minced)

1/4 cup fresh cilantro (chopped)
salt and freshly ground black pepper

Method
1. In a small bowl, combine the white wine, olive oil, ginger, garlic, and cilantro. Season with salt and pepper. Mix well.
2. Now, the marinade is ready to use.
3. Pour mixture onto your chicken or fish and marinate for at least 1-2 hours to absorb flavors.

◆◆◆◆◆◆◆◆

Les Ilagan

Easy Teriyaki Marinade

This is the probably the best teriyaki marinade that you will ever have.

Preparation time: 5 minutes
Total time: 5 minutes
Yield: 1 1/2 cups

Ingredients

1/2 cup mirin (Japanese sweet rice wine)
1/2 cup soy sauce
1/3 cup brown sugar
3 cloves garlic (minced)

1 shallot (minced)
1 teaspoon fresh ginger (minced)
1 teaspoon sesame oil
1/4 teaspoon freshly ground black pepper

Method

1. Bring mirin, soy sauce, brown sugar to a boil in a medium saucepan over medium-high heat. Cook for 3 minutes.

2. Meanwhile, combine cornstarch and water in a small bowl until dissolved completely.

3. Stir in cornstarch mixture, garlic, shallot, ginger, and black pepper. Cook further3 minutes. Add sesame oil and stir well. Remove from heat. Allow to cool.

4. Now, the marinade is ready to use.

5. Pour mixture onto your meat or chicken and marinate for at least 1-2 hours to absorb flavors.

♦♦♦♦♦♦♦♦

Spicy Vegetable Marinade

Your marinated vegetables will never be the same without this spicy marinade recipe!

Preparation time: 5 minutes
Total time: 5 minutes
Yield: 1 cup

Ingredients

2/3 cup apple cider vinegar
1/3 cup olive oil
1 red hot chili pepper (chopped)

1 teaspoon fresh ginger (finely grated)
1 teaspoon of garlic powder
1/2 teaspoon of black pepper
salt to taste

Method

1. In a small bowl, combine the apple cider vinegar, olive oil, chili, ginger, garlic, and black pepper. Season with salt, to taste. Mix well.

2. Now, the marinade is ready to use.

3. Pour mixture onto your vegetables and marinate for at least 1-2 hours to absorb flavors.

◆◆◆◆◆◆◆◆◆

Soya Herb and Garlic Marinade

This soya based marinade recipe with herbs and garlic goes well with any kind of grilled meat.

Preparation time: 5 minutes
Total time: 5 minutes
Yield: 1 cup

Ingredients
1/2 cup soy sauce

1/3 cup rice wine vinegar
1/4 cup brown sugar
1 teaspoon garlic (minced)
1/2 teaspoon dried coriander
1/2 teaspoon dried thyme
1/2 teaspoon freshly ground black pepper

Method

1. In a small bowl, combine the soy sauce, rice wine vinegar, brown sugar, garlic, coriander, thyme, and black pepper. Mix well.
2. Now, the marinade is ready to use.
3. Pour mixture onto your meat and marinate for at least 1-2 hours to absorb flavors.

◆◆◆◆◆◆◆◆

Spicy Grilled Chicken Marinade

This spicy marinade is can be used on grilled poultry or meat.

Preparation Time: 5 minutes
Total Time: 5 minutes
Yield: 1 cup

Ingredients
1/3 cup soy sauce
1/4 cup of rice vinegar
1/4 cup water
1/3 cup brown sugar
1 teaspoon chili powder
1 teaspoon cumin (ground)

1/2 teaspoon ginger (ground)
1/2 teaspoon onion powder
1/2 teaspoon garlic powder
salt and freshly ground black pepper

Method

1. Whisk together the soy sauce, rice vinegar, water, and brown sugar in a small saucepan. Bring to a boil over high heat. Reduce heat and simmer for 5 minutes. Remove from heat.
2. Stir in the chili powder, cumin, ginger, onion powder, and garlic powder. Season with salt and pepper, to taste. Allowto cool.
3. Now, the marinade is ready to use.
4. Pour mixture onto your chicken and marinate for at least 1-2 hours to absorb flavors.

♦♦♦♦♦♦♦♦

Les Ilagan

Yogurt and Citrus Marinade with Coriander

The yogurt and citrus will not only enhance the flavor of your meat but will also make them tender.

Preparation time: 5 minutes
Total time: 5 minutes
Yield: 1 1/4 cups

Ingredients

3/4 cup plain yogurt
2 tablespoons honey
2 tablespoons lemon juice

1 tablespoon lemon zest (finely grated)
1 teaspoon garlic (minced)
¼ cup fresh coriander (chopped)
salt and freshly ground black pepper

Method

1. Whisk together the yogurt, honey, lemon juice, zest, garlic, and coriander in a small bowl. Season with salt and pepper, to taste. Allow to cool.

2. Now, the marinade is ready to use.

3. Pour mixture onto your meat and marinate for at least 1-2 hours to absorb flavors.

♦♦♦♦♦♦♦♦

Les Ilagan

Sweet and Spicy Barbecue Marinade

This marinade goes well with flank steak, New York strip, or filet mignon.

Preparation time: 5 minutes
Total time: 5 minutes
Yield: 1 cup

Ingredients

1/2 cup ketchup
1/2cup brown sugar

1/4 cup soy sauce
2 tablespoons vegetable oil
1 tablespoon Worcestershire sauce
1 tablespoon chili paste
1 teaspoon sweet paprika
½ teaspoon cumin (ground)
½ teaspoon coriander (ground)
salt and freshly ground black pepper

Method

1. Combine the ketchup, brown sugar, soy sauce, vegetable oil, Worcestershire sauce, chili paste, paprika, cumin, and coriander in a small bowl. Season with salt and pepper, to taste. Mix well.
2. Now, the marinade is ready to use.
3. Pour mixture onto your meat and marinate for at least 1-2 hours to absorb flavors.

♦♦♦♦♦♦♦♦

Les Ilagan

Lemon Ginger and Garlic Fish Marinade

This simple marinade with lemon, ginger, and garlic is perfect for marinating fish and seafood.

Preparation time: 5 minutes
Total time: 5 minutes
Yield: 1 cup

Ingredients

2/3 cup lemon juice
1/4 cup olive oil
1 shallot (thinly sliced)

2 tablespoons fresh mixed herbs (chopped)
1 tablespoon fresh ginger (grated)
1 tablespoon garlic (minced)
1 tablespoon whole peppercorns
1 teaspoon sugar
salt and freshly ground black pepper

Method

1. Whisk together the lemon juice, olive oil, shallot, mixed herbs, ginger, garlic, peppercorns, and sugar in a small bowl. Season with salt and pepper, to taste. Mix well.
2. Now, the marinade is ready to use.
3. Pour mixture onto your fish and marinate for at least 1-2 hours to absorb flavors.

♦♦♦♦♦♦♦♦

Les Ilagan

Maple Lime and Herb Marinade

This tasty marinade is perfect for steaks, chicken fillets, or lamb chops!

Preparation time: 5 minutes
Total time: 5 minutes
Yield: 1 cup

Ingredients

1/2 cup lime juice
1/3 cup maple syrup
2 tablespoons olive oil

½ teaspoon dried thyme
½ teaspoon dried sage
½ teaspoon dried rosemary
salt and freshly ground black pepper

Method

1. Whisk together the lime juice, maple syrup, olive oil, thyme, sage, and rosemary in a small bowl. Season with salt and pepper, to taste. Mix well.
2. Now, the marinade is ready to use.
3. Pour mixture onto your meat or chicken and marinate for at least 1-2 hours to absorb flavors.

♦♦♦♦♦♦♦♦♦

Sun-Dried Tomato Marinade with Garlic and Herb

This Mediterranean-inspired marinade goes well with vegetables, meat, fish, or poultry.

Preparation time: 5 minutes
Total time: 5 minutes
Yield: 1 1/4 cup

Ingredients

1/2 cup olive oil
1/4 cup sun-dried tomatoes
2 tablespoons tomato paste

2 tablespoons balsamic vinegar
1 teaspoon sweet paprika
1 teaspoon cumin (ground)
1 tablespoon garlic (chopped)
¼ cup fresh parsley (chopped)
salt and freshly ground black pepper

Method

1. Combine the olive oil, sun-dried tomatoes, tomato paste, balsamic vinegar, paprika, and cumin in a food processor. Process until smooth. Transfer in a small bowl.

2. Stir in garlic and parsley. Season with salt and pepper, to taste.

3. Now, the marinade is ready to use.

4. Pour mixture onto vegetables, meat, fish, or poultry then marinate for at least 1-2 hours.

♦♦♦♦♦♦♦♦

Made in the USA
Lexington, KY
15 December 2016